MW01199098

1

♥ LOVE is Patient ♥ LOVE is Kind ♥ LOVE does not Envy ♥
♥ LOVE does not Boast ♥ LOVE is not Proud ♥ LOVE is not Rude ♥
♥ LOVE is not Self Seeking ♥ LOVE is not Easily Angered ♥
♥ LOVE keeps no record of Wrongs ♥
♥ LOVE does not delight in Evil ♥ LOVE rejoices with the Truth ♥
♥ LOVE always Protects ♥ LOVE always Trusts ♥ LOVE always Hopes ♥
♥ LOVE always Preserves ♥ LOVE never Fails ♥

1 Corinthians 13:4-8

The 16 Day
Love Challenge
1 Corinthians 13:4~8

Matching our
Words and
Actions
with
1 Corinthians
13:4-8

Cherie L. Zack ♥ Rebecca LeCompte
two imperfect wives

Copyright © 2013 by Cherie Zack & Rebecca LeCompte.

Published by The Imperfect Wives
P.O.Box 2161
Beaufort, SC 29901

All rights reserved. No portion of this publication may be reproduced, stored in a retrieval system or transmitted in any form by any means—except for brief quotations in published reviews—without the prior written permission of the authors.

All scripture quotations, unless otherwise indicated, are taken from the Holy Bible, New International Version®, NIV®. Copyright ©1973, 1978, 1984, 2011 by Biblica, Inc. ™ Used by permission of Zondervan. All rights reserved worldwide. www.zondervan.com The "NIV" and "New International Version" are trademarks registered in the United States Patent and Trademark Office by Biblica, Inc. ™

The "NIV" and "New International Version" are trademarks registered in the United States Patent and Trademark Office by Biblica, Inc. ™

The ESV® Bible (The Holy Bible, English Standard Version®) copyright © 2001 by Crossway, a publishing ministry of Good News Publishers. ESV® Text Edition: 2011. The ESV® text has been reproduced in cooperation with and by permission of Good News Publishers. Unauthorized reproduction of this publication is prohibited. All rights reserved.

"Scripture taken from the New King James Version®. Copyright © 1982 by Thomas Nelson, Inc. Used by permission. All rights reserved."

The Authorized (King James) Version of the Bible ('the KJV'), the rights in which are vested in the Crown in the United Kingdom, is reproduced here by permission of the Crown's patentee, Cambridge University Press.

This is dedicated to every woman that has struggled with past issues concerning love. Every little girl deserves to be loved and cherished by her daddy. God designed this relationship between father and daughter to be the conduit between us and Him. Little girls who grow up without a loving daddy are sometimes dealt a harsh blow and can struggle for years to understand why or how God loves them. My prayer is this, that God can open a door through each challenge allowing you to find courage and strength and begin to receive His great love for you. Lay down every hindrance and let God embrace you today.

> With love,
> Cherie

This book is also dedicated to all of our friends who call themselves imperfect wives with us. Your sisterhood with us as we discuss our faith, the great love that has been shown through Jesus Christ, and our marriages is a gift that we cherish beyond our ability to express in mere words. You are a treasure in our lives and it is our privilege to be on this journey with you.

> With love,
> Rebecca

Table of Contents

We would like to thank

First -all of the women in The Imperfect Wives Club. We could not have written this book without you, your transparency is inspiring. Thank you for letting God use you the way He has designed you. We love you!

Deborah Sewell, thank you for the many hours of prayer you have prayed over this project and over us! You are invaluable to us and our ministries.

Sarah Schindler, for the many hours of formatting and reformatting you gave to get this book ready to print. God brought you to us at the right time! We are so blessed to have you. Please know you are greatly appreciated and loved! There is no one like you!

Bill, Rob, and our children, for giving us the time to write together. Thank you for believing in us to write this project. Most of what we have written is based on what we have learned from all of you. We love you greatly.

And most importantly, we acknowledge that without God giving us the courage to step out in faith and share some of our intimate stories, this study wouldn't have happened.

Reviews

Cherie and Rebecca bring a beautiful, refreshing, perspective to the Love chapter of 1 Corinthians 13. You will see LOVE like you've never seen it before! This study will change the hearts of women everywhere!

Karen M. Jantzi, CPLC
Founder & Executive Director
TREASURED WOMAN LLC

The 16 Day Love Challenge will strengthen your Love walk with all you encounter. I am so thankful for the leadership Cherie and Rebecca offer through this study to every wife. It is my privilege to recommend the 16 Day Love Challenge.

Leanne Collins

I love this challenge. I love the way it amplifies each aspect of what love really means. I gained understanding and practical ways to apply the Word to my life and my marriage. I highly recommend it to wives and those who desire to be married. Thank you, Cherie Zack & Rebecca LeCompte for the loving labor that went into this challenge. Looking forward to more.

Deborah Sewell

Foreword

Have you ever attended a marriage seminar or heard an insightful sermon on marriage and found yourself hoping your husband was listening—wanting **him** to get it? I know I have. Most of us have fallen into the trap of wanting our husbands or others around us to change. Maybe we've even thought, *if they would change,* **then** *I could change, and our relationship would be much easier...*

The truth is—those types of thoughts are a waste of mental energy and produce unhealthy attitudes. Critical attitudes eventually create behaviors, which can alienate us from the people in our lives, generating even more negative emotions. We can actually become trapped in a vicious cycle leading us to discouragement and despair.

Those thoughts can also keep us focused in the wrong direction, causing us to neglect the opportunities to change the one person we can actually change— ourselves! When we take our eyes off of the ways we hope others will change, we can give our attention to growing more Christ-like. His desire for each of us is to love others the way He loves us. (And by the way, becoming more loving will positively impact others much more than nagging or simply wishing they were different. *Love* changes people!)

Cherie and Rebecca have provided a simple, yet profound 16-day challenge from First Corinthians chapter 13. With the help of the Holy Spirit, we can grow in our understanding of God's amazing love for us, and our ability to demonstrate that same love to others. It is the kind of self-sacrificing love Jesus has for us, a love that wants what is best for the other person—it is patient, kind, trusting, and hopeful. It doesn't envy or boast. It is not easily angered or critical. It is the kind of love that perseveres, protects, and never gives up. As you walk through this challenge, I pray God will reveal His perfect love for you in fresh, new ways and that your joy will be complete as you love others!

- Kerry Clarensau, Speaker and Author
Kerry is the Director of a national women's organization that numbers over 340,000 members. She is a credentialed minister, a mentor, and an international speaker. A prolific writer, she creates

resources for ministry to women and is the author of *Secrets: Transforming Your Life and Marriage, Love Revealed,* and *Redeemed: Embracing a Transformed Life.*

God Is Love

Cherie:

I had only been married 2 years when God began to draw my attention to *His design* for us. We were stationed in Newport News, Virginia at the time of my story. This was our first duty station as husband and wife.

We met lots of people and made new friends quickly. One of my friends was having a Home Interior party {remember these?} and had invited me. While at the party my eyes were drawn to a print that simply said, "Love is patient, Love is kind, Love does not envy," and included six more love attributes. My thought was that I could hang it above our bed and be reminded that God loves us.

Most of the party-goers lived in our apartment complex so we planned to reunite on the day our orders came in. I had spent many days with my thoughts going back to the print and could not wait to hang it, and the day had finally come.

Everyone arrived and we were excited to see what we had ordered. It seemed more like a baby or wedding shower than it did a Home Interior party. We watched as everyone opened their boxes to reveal the treasures hidden inside. Soon we realized that many of us ordered the same print.

I was so excited to open my box. As I did, I noticed something fell out of it. It was a small piece of paper that simply read,

Bill is patient

Bill is kind

Bill does not envy

Bill does not boast.....

I was surprised to see *Bill* instead of love. Intrigued, I asked my friends if they had the same small piece of paper included with their prints. They each looked and said yes. I then asked them what the paper said. One by one they said, "Mine says Love."

Wow! Mine said Bill. This is not just another name to me. It is the name my mother-in- law gave her youngest child and the man I married.

Do you think God was trying to get my attention from the start? Why was it so important that I understood "love" so early in my marriage? I can safely say I'm not a woman who believes in coincidence. I have come to learn that God's timing is everything. He loves us so much that He will orchestrate moments in our life that we cannot mistake for something other than His perfect design.

*"For whatever things were written before were written for our learning, that we through the **patience** and comfort of the Scriptures might have hope."* Romans 15:4 (NKJV)

Rebecca:

I grew up with this oh-so-familiar passage of scripture on a plaque on the wall of my parents' home. As a girl,

I liked these words, but honestly didn't give them too much thought...they simply became part of the backdrop.

After Robert and I married, I began to pay a bit more attention to these words, mostly because I became acutely aware of how poorly I compared to this standard. I wasn't very patient, kind, *or* trusting. God revealed to me how incapable I was of truly loving Robert in my own strength of will or depth of emotion.

I really needed to grow up in the Lord!

The good news for me, Robert, and our family is that God didn't leave me to wrestle alone with my shortcomings. For that, I am eternally grateful!

The Lord gave me His precious Holy Spirit and began to teach me how to genuinely love Robert and others as He loves them, even when my emotions, circumstances, and thoughts didn't naturally lend themselves to loving words and actions. It wasn't an overnight process, but I always had hope because God enabled me to have steady progress.

And hope does not disappoint us, because God has poured out his love into our hearts by the Holy Spirit, whom he has given us. Romans 5:5 (NIV)

Dear Friend,

Welcome to this beautiful, challenging journey with us!

Loving intensely is a highly personal, and usually private, endeavor. However, we have felt the Spirit of the Living God call us to share our journey and some of the lessons we have learned along the way. We are still students, learning new lessons from our loving Daddy every day.

We pray that as you journey with us, you will feel the presence of God and hear His voice whispering encouragement to love your husband {and others} more deeply. We pray that you give your love unconditionally, with no strings attached, despite your emotions and circumstances. Lastly, we pray that as you continue, you find your passion for God and for loving others reignited and it burns more brightly and steadily than ever before.

Cherie & Rebecca

Chapter 1

Love Is Patient

"Love is patient, love is kind. It does not envy, it does not boast, it is not proud. It does not dishonor others, it is not self-seeking, it is not easily angered, it keeps no record of wrongs. Love does not delight in evil but rejoices with the truth. It always protects, always trusts, always hopes, always perseveres. Love never fails."

-1 Corinthians 13:4-8 (NIV)

Love is Patient! We know the words....

It's no accident that patience is the first attribute of love in this passage. Patience is foundational to the rest of the characteristics listed here. Without patience, one cannot be kind. Without patience, there is envy, boasting and pride. When patience is absent, rudeness, self-seeking and anger abound. Impatience allows for keeping track of wrongs and delighting in evil rather than rejoicing with the truth. The motivation to protect, trust, hope and persevere leaves when there is a lack of patience. Patience is *vital* to our ability to love those around us! Because it is so important, patience has come under attack in a unique way.

How many times have we heard *not* to pray for increased patience because we will end up facing trying circumstances? In fact, it's the *only* aspect of love that we've been warned not to pray for. We choose to work apart from God and operate in our own power. We kick patience to the curb, laugh at it, and walk on our merry way, convinced that we can handle whatever gets thrown at us. Then, reality hits and we realize that we are ill-equipped to handle the storms of life.

But God offers us hope. Once we're born again, the Holy Spirit lives inside us and gives us the strength we need to endure. We must embrace James 1:4 which says, "*But let patience have its perfect work.*" Let's take a good look at James 1:2-4,

"My brethren, count it all joy when you fall into various trials, knowing that the testing of your faith produces patience. But let patience have its perfect work, that you may be perfect and complete, lacking nothing." (NIV)

What stands out to you? Maybe you caught that patience takes time to develop as it's tested. It doesn't happen overnight. It takes a variety of circumstances to improve and refine patience. As patience develops, it changes you through its *perfect* work. The NIV says it this way, "Let perseverance finish its work so that you may be mature and complete, not lacking anything."

If we stop to think about these verses, we see a "patience cycle" that looks like this:

1. You face a trial or test of your faith.
2. That test works on your patience, or perseverance, strengthening this characteristic in you.
3. At the end of that test, if you have been successful, you are more mature than you were at the beginning.
4. Go back to #1 and start again on the next (probably different) trial or test of your faith.

Rebecca's story:

When our sons were young, family dinners became the place where my lack of patience became painfully evident. I was consistently impatient with Robert concerning his interaction with the boys. Instead of simply enjoying our times of family togetherness, I would focus on what I perceived as Robert's weaknesses as a parent. My impatience with him ruined many evenings as I chose criticism over kindness, humility, and love.

Finally I listened to the Holy Spirit, who told me to excuse myself from the table if I couldn't keep my mouth shut! He gave me another option, too: to simply place my hand over my mouth so I wouldn't speak. For a season, dinners at our house were pretty quiet as I strove to obey by being silent. During that season of quiet, I was able to hear the Holy Spirit's voice tell me that I needed to praise Robert's parenting efforts and pray for him in areas as HE directed me (not as I thought in my own wisdom). The outcome of this obedience was increased patience in me. I honestly can't tell you how much Robert changed through those circumstances, but I know that I became more patient as a result of that test! (And I know for certain that Robert is glad I passed!)

Today's Challenge:

Have you ignored the "patience" aspect of love? No? Give God a minute. He will reveal it to you!

Who in your life have you consistently hurt because of your lack of patience? Your husband, your child, a co-worker, your friend, or a loved one? Write down his or her name and what you see that impatience has cost you in this relationship. Now, share this story with God and ask for forgiveness.

Secondly, choose patience over your "I got this" way of thinking. Ask God to line your thoughts up with His word. Patience needs to exist within us to allow the other characteristics of love to be made manifest in our lives. ♥ Cherie & Rebecca

Day 1 ~ Love is Patient

_____
_____
_____
_____
_____
_____
_____
_____
_____
_____
_____
_____
_____
_____
_____
_____
_____
_____
_____
_____
_____
_____
_____
_____
_____
_____
_____
_____
_____
_____
_____
_____
_____
_____
_____

"My brethren, count it all joy when you fall into various trials, knowing that the testing of your faith produces patience. But let patience have its perfect work, that you may be perfect and complete, lacking nothing." -James 1:2-4 (NIV)

Chapter 2

Love Is Kind

"At one time we too were foolish, disobedient, deceived and enslaved by all kinds of passions and pleasures. We lived in malice and envy, being hated and hating one another. But when the kindness and love of God our Savior appeared, he saved us, not because of righteous things we had done, but because of his mercy. He saved us through the washing of rebirth and renewal by the Holy Spirit, whom he poured out on us generously through Jesus Christ our Savior..."

-Titus 3:3-6 (NIV)

Kindness can be described as having the qualities of being friendly, generous, and considerate.

God is so kind to us! Because of His kindness to us, we had the opportunity to be saved. He reached out to us first, being "friendly" to us when we were strangers with Him.

God is generous with us. He owns everything and has control over the universe. He chooses to give us life and then sustain that life, even to the wonderful extent that He gives us eternal life. He provides for our needs on a consistent, ongoing basis, whether we deserve it or not. It's all His to give and He gives generously. James 1:5 says that God even gives His wisdom generously to all without finding fault. That is a wonderful gift, considering this interaction between God and Solomon in 2 Chronicles 1:7-12:

> That night God appeared to Solomon and said to him, "Ask for whatever you want me to give you." Solomon answered God, "You have shown great **kindness** to David my father and have made me king in his place. Now, LORD God, let your promise to my father David be confirmed, for you have made me king over a people who are as numerous as the dust of the earth. Give me wisdom and knowledge, that I may lead this people, for who is able to govern this great people of yours?"
>
> God said to Solomon, "Since this is your heart's desire and you have not asked for wealth, riches or honor, nor for the death of your enemies, and since you have not asked for a long life but for wisdom and knowledge to govern my people over whom I have made you king, therefore wisdom and knowledge will be given you. And I will also give you wealth, riches and honor, such as no king who was before you ever had and none after you will have." (NIV)

God is considerate. He's supremely attentive to us and our needs, mindful of what is best for us at all times. 1 John 4:8b says, "God is love." If God is love and love is kind, then it stands to reason that God is kind. God is the embodiment of true kindness.

God's kindness in saving us from our own sin wasn't dependent upon our first exhibiting kindness toward Him. For that, I am forever grateful!

Often, it is tempting to let another's behavior be our standard for our own actions and words. When others are kind, kindness is easily returned. However, when met with an unkind attitude it can be a different story, especially when the unkind person is someone close to you, like a husband, family member or friend.

When unkindness is a regular issue in a relationship, it can be a difficult pattern to break. There's good news, though. To see real change, all it takes is one person willing to be kind...friendly, generous, and considerate...NO MATTER WHAT the other person does. Are you willing to be that person?

Today's Challenge:

Thank God for His (undeserved) kindness toward you.

Ask God to show you where you have been unkind toward your husband or someone close to you. Confess your sin and repent. God is faithful and just to cleanse you from that unrighteousness.

Ask yourself if you are really willing to be kind no matter what. If the answer is yes, tell the Lord that you've made that decision and ask Him to anoint you to display HIS kindness toward your husband (and everyone else!). ♥ Rebecca

Day 2 ~ Love is Kind

_____
_____
_____
_____
_____
_____
_____
_____
_____
_____
_____
_____
_____
_____
_____
_____
_____
_____
_____
_____
_____
_____
_____
_____
_____

*"God is so kind to us! Because of His kindness to us,
we had the opportunity to be saved. He reached out
to us first, being "friendly" to us when we were
strangers with Him." - Rebecca LeCompte*

Chapter 3

Love Does Not Envy

"Search me, O God, and know my heart; Try me, and
know my anxieties; and see if there is any wicked way
in me, And lead me in the way everlasting."

-Psalm 139:23-24 (NIV)

Envy is a feeling of discontent or covetousness with regard to another's advantages, success, possessions, etc. (Definition from Dictionary.com)

I have dealt with envy. It started when Bill was deployed on the John F. Kennedy in 1997. He was bound for the Mediterranean Sea for a 7-month deployment and I was home alone taking care of our 4 children, including one with cerebral palsy and a seizure disorder. When the days got hard I found myself envying Bill and his ability to be oblivious to what I was dealing with in our everyday life. In time this envy turned into jealousy and then bitterness.

I'm sure some of you are thinking that I had a right to be frustrated. After all, I was left with a heavy load.

Frustration alone isn't a sin if we give it to God and let Him walk us through it. The issue with my envy of Bill and his ability to be clueless turned into sin when I allowed it to take priority in my thought life. This sin opened the door to other sins creating an even larger problem. Bill had no idea that I had become so envious of him.

James 3:16 says *"For where jealousy and selfish ambition exist, there will be disorder and every vile practice."* All of a sudden *disorder* had become my middle name. My thoughts were out of order and beyond my control, giving way to jealousy and an unsound mind. Believe me when I tell you that I was a *hot mess!*

Did you know that envy and jealousy go hand in hand? Envy can take us down the wrong road if we don't stop it in its tracks. Who do you envy? Perhaps you are envious of a friend at work. A co-worker's good news can be a stumbling block for many. Maybe you're envious of your husband and the favor God has given him. You can see his light shining while you are waiting for your own time to shine. There are many reasons why we can find ourselves envying others. However, Paul teaches us that love and envy don't mix.

My life verse is Psalm 27:4 which says,

"One thing I ask from the LORD, this only do I seek: that I may dwell in the house of the LORD all the days of my life, to gaze on the beauty of the LORD and to seek him in his temple."

In the meantime, my desire to draw near to God had gotten to the point of desperation and yet I could not seem to find the right entrance into His presence. Eventually I learned that *envy* had become a stumbling block for me and was keeping me from gaining access to the very place I longed to be. I had to remove this before I could fully enter His temple. Why? Because He wants *all of me*. My envy of Bill put a barrier between God and me and I had to be willing to let go and let God have control.

Today's Challenge:

My sweet sisters, search your hearts. Does envy reside there? If so, submit each area of envy to God and ask Him to redeem you and all that it has taken. Warning: if envy is a stronghold for you, satan will fight to keep his territory. Start with acknowledging God and invite Him into the process. He longs to refine and free you from every sin, including envy, allowing *love* to flow freely once again. ♥ Cherie

Day 3 ~ Love does not Envy

_____
_____
_____
_____
_____
_____
_____
_____
_____
_____
_____
_____
_____
_____
_____
_____
_____
_____
_____
_____
_____
_____
_____
_____
_____
_____
_____

"For where jealousy and selfish ambition exist, there will be disorder and every vile practice." - James 3:16

Chapter 4

Love Does Not Boast

"When we put bits into the mouths of horses to make them obey us, we can turn the whole animal. Or take ships as an example. Although they are so large and are driven by strong winds, they are steered by a very small rudder wherever the pilot wants to go. Likewise the tongue is a small part of the body, but it makes great boasts. Consider what a great forest is set on fire by a small spark. The tongue also is a fire, a world of evil among the parts of the body. It corrupts the whole person, sets the whole course of his life on fire, and is itself set on fire by hell."

-James 3:3-6 (NIV)

Love doesn't "talk about itself with excessive pride or self-satisfaction about achievements, possessions, or abilities." (Definition from Oxford American Dictionaries)

Consider this passage found in Luke 18:9-14,

To some who were confident of their own righteousness and looked down on everybody else, Jesus told this parable: "Two men went up to the temple to pray, one a Pharisee and the other a tax

45

collector. The Pharisee stood up and prayed about
himself: 'God, I thank you that I am not like other
men—robbers, evildoers, adulterers—or even like this
tax collector. I fast twice a week and give a tenth of
all I get.'
"But the tax collector stood at a distance. He would
not even look up to heaven, but beat his breast and
said, 'God, have mercy on me, a sinner.'
"I tell you that this man, rather than the other, went
home justified before God. For everyone who exalts
himself will be humbled, and he who humbles himself
will be exalted." (NIV)

The sin of boasting shows itself first in thoughts rather than in words. The evil twins of comparison and competition enter our thoughts as we measure our achievements as a spouse, parent, friend, employee, or Christian against the accomplishments of others.

There are a couple of main ways that process of boasting begins. I'm sure there are more, but for today, let's examine these two:

If we believe that the person we're comparing ourselves to is weaker than we are in a particular area, we find ourselves mentally patting ourselves on the back as we come out "on top" in that comparison. Whether we mean to or not, often those thoughts come out in our words as we gloat about our success in a particular area of life, proclaiming ourselves experts in a particular domain.

Sometimes we begin that process of comparison and believe that we are falling short. When we find

ourselves there, we can fall prey to the fear that others
see our shortcomings and begin our campaign of
boastful comments, often exaggerating our results in
order to camouflage or perceived faults.

Once we take the bait of comparison, we often find
ourselves engaged in an undeclared competition with
a person and end up in a vicious cycle of alternating
comparative and competitive thoughts.

Maybe we don't say these things to others, but "pray"
them like the Pharisee in Luke 18. Or maybe we
choose to say them to a third party, building ourselves
up in their eyes while diminishing the object of our
comparison/competition. As it says in Luke 18:14, if
we will humble ourselves (instead of boasting) we will
find ourselves exalted by God.

Love chooses to speak with humility about ourselves
instead of boasting. Love builds up others. Love does
not compare or compete with others, but sees them as
God sees them, with no need to exalt itself.

Today's Challenge:

Go back and read today's scriptures again and take
note of what stands out to you.

Repent of your boasting.

Ask the Lord to help you to identify comparison and
competition in your thoughts and speech so that you
can take a stand against this scheme of the enemy.
When you feel tempted to boast about yourself (or
become aware that you have already given in to that

temptation), choose to fight that by boasting in the Lord and all that He has done for you.

Another weapon that you can use to fight the temptation to boast about yourself is to then turn around and boast about that other person to God, to yourself, and to others. Hearing yourself honor that person's achievements, gifting's, and skills puts things back into the right perspective in your thought life, eliminating the competition. (Remember that you are *never* diminished by someone else's accomplishments!) ♥ Rebecca

Day 4 ~ Love does not Boast

_____
_____
_____
_____
_____
_____
_____
_____
_____
_____
_____
_____
_____
_____
_____
_____
_____
_____
_____
_____
_____
_____
_____
_____
_____
_____
_____
_____
_____

"Love chooses to speak with humility about ourselves instead of boasting. Love builds up others. Love does not compare or compete with others, but sees them as God sees them, with no need to exalt itself." -Rebecca LeCompte

49

Chapter 5

Love Is Not Proud

"Do nothing out of selfish ambition or vain conceit,
but in humility consider others better than
yourselves." -Philippians 2:3 (NIV)

Pride always comes before the fall. We understand
how easy it can be to get caught up in pride. A "job
well done" from our boss, God using us to share a
word of knowledge with someone or overcoming a
personal struggle that we have been fighting with for
years are all things that can cause us to get the *big
head* syndrome if we don't stay balanced in our
thinking and focused on Jesus and His desire to use
us.

Pride tells us we are greater than those around us.
Pride gives way to judging others based on our own
self-worth. Proverbs 25:27 says, "*It is not good to eat
much honey;
So to seek one's own glory is not glory.*" Just as too
much honey makes the body sick, pride makes the
spirit sick. To see others through God's eyes is a
natural reflection of perfect love, God's love.

Without the right understanding of God and His love for people, our arrogance will continue to develop until we suffer the consequences of our pride. The Bible states in James 4:6 that *God resists the proud but gives grace to the humble.* I think we can all agree that pride is not the direction God wants us to go. After all, the expression of *pride* is the absence of *love.*

Today's Challenge:

Pride seeks self glory but love seeks God's glory. Ask God to reveal the areas where pride has invaded your heart and separated you from your husband, friends, coworkers, neighbors, and family members -any relationship where you have allowed pride to become a barrier between you and them. Lay this before the cross and ask God to teach you how to replace pride with love. It takes humility to stand in the face of pride and repent. God has promised us in James 4:10 that as we humble ourselves in His sight, He will lift us up. Sweet sisters, let God lift you today. ♥ Cherie

Day 5 ~ Love is not Proud

_____
_____
_____
_____
_____
_____
_____
_____
_____
_____
_____
_____
_____
_____
_____
_____
_____
_____
_____
_____
_____
_____
_____
_____
_____
_____
_____
_____
_____
_____
_____

"Pride seeks self glory but love seeks God's glory." - Cherie Zack

Chapter 6

Love Is Not Rude

"He who loves a pure heart and whose speech is
gracious will have the king for his friend."
-Proverbs 22:11 (NIV)

Rude means offensively impolite or ill-mannered, discourteous, disrespectful, curt, short, uncivil, impertinent, impudent, sharp, insulting, derogatory, disparaging, abusive, tactless, undiplomatic, uncomplimentary. (Definition from Oxford American Dictionaries)

That means that love is NOT any of those things!

Love is polite. When we act in loving ways toward others, we are courteous...we use our manners. Love is tactful, gracious, and deals with people in sensitive ways. Maybe you see yourself in this description: very polite with friends, co-workers, people at church, and strangers in the marketplace. Then, behind closed doors you suddenly find yourself in a battle to be polite to your family, especially at times when you feel frustrated, tired, or stressed.

I remember when God first revealed that contrast in my own behavior. My young sons were being rude to each other on a fairly consistent basis. As I began to correct them, the Lord showed me that they had learned that from me. I was so convicted and wept bitterly at that revelation of my sin.

At first, I wondered what was wrong with me, but the Holy Spirit showed me how very common this is. He told me that the "disconnect" in my behavior was because I was letting my guard down. When I was alone with my family, I spoke in irritated, frustrated tones (or worse), without stopping to consider the impact I was having on my family.

That was many years ago and I am pleased to announce that the vast majority of the time, my boys and I are polite to each other, even behind closed doors. But, when we are tired or stressed, rudeness is still a temptation. We had victory within just a few short weeks all those years ago because we focused our attention on being polite with one another, immediately identified rude speech and then practiced polite speech on the spot. That type of practice was extremely effective! We also understand the value of maintenance in this area so we are quick to correct ourselves and the boys are still willing to receive instruction when they stumble in this area. (Our sons are 21 and 17 now, so we've been working on this for more than 15 years!)

I share this story so that you can have hope that lasting change is possible and attainable when you submit to God. My sons and I have had to humble ourselves in order to become and stay polite in our home. The sense of peace that comes from our courtesy with each other is priceless!

I don't think it's any accident that rude has so many synonyms. It reminds me of Matthew 7:13-14, which say,

"Enter through the narrow gate. For wide is the gate and broad is the road that leads to destruction, and many enter through it. But small is the gate and narrow the road that leads to life, and only a few find it." (NIV)

The "wide gate" is all of the things that are rude. The "narrow gate" is the way of love.

Today's Challenge:

Have you been rude to someone in your life recently? Repent and then prayerfully consider apologizing to them. You might be pleasantly surprised by their gracious response to this kind of expression of remorse.

Choose to be loving by being polite and gracious with others. Remember that God is never curt, short, uncivil, or impolite to us...even when we deserve it. God is always LOVING in His attitude toward us, even when disciplining us.

Ask God to reveal to you phrases, habits, attitudes, body language, facial expressions, or anything at all that conveys an attitude of rudeness instead of love. As He does, remember that these revelations are not for the sake of condemnation, but because He loves you and wants you to be changed from glory to glory so that you can better reflect His love to those around you. He does not want you to change in order to diminish you, but to give you even more abundance in life. As you lay down things that are not bearing good fruit in your life, you will begin to see a greater harvest of righteousness. ♥ Rebecca

Day 6 ~ Love is not Rude

_____
_____
_____
_____
_____
_____
_____
_____
_____
_____
_____
_____
_____
_____
_____
_____
_____
_____
_____
_____
_____
_____
_____
_____
_____
_____
_____
_____
_____
_____
_____
_____
_____
_____

"He who loves a pure heart and whose speech is gracious will have the king for his friend." -Proverbs 22:11 (NIV)

Chapter 7

Love Is Not Self-seeking

"But for those who are self-seeking and who reject the truth and follow evil, there will be wrath and anger."
Romans 2:8 (NIV)

Self-seeking means the seeking of one's own interest or selfish ends. (Definition from Dictionary.com)

Have you found yourself in a place where every decision you make is to cover yourself or to further your own plan, leaving behind God or those in your life? The Bible tells us to deny ourselves and lay down our lives for others.

Why are we selfish? Is it because we feel we are lacking and deserve to have what we feel should be ours? Could it be out of self-preservation or an addiction? Maybe it is because fear is in control. I think sometimes it's that we want what we want, plain and simple, and brush God off instead of submitting to Him like we should.

I have a close friend who is addicted to drugs. Those of us who love him came together back in 2010 to hold an intervention. Our prayer was that we could reach him through our expressed love and he would understand what he was losing because of the addiction. Things did not go quite the way we had hoped. He stated to us that he wasn't ready to walk away from the drugs. But we had a card we could use that we were sure would get his attention.

We reminded him of his son who was only 8 at the time. We shared with him that he was putting his own life is great danger and could ultimately leave his son fatherless. His response shocked every single one of us. He said, "_____ can find another dad!"

Obviously the most important aspect missing from him was love. By sharing this, he said his love for the drugs was much greater than the love he had for his son. The desire for self-seeking had replaced love and he chose to follow evil instead of receiving the truth. To this day he is still in the same place.

Today's Challenge:
Are you self-seeking? Though it may not be to the same depth as my friend's, any form of self-seeking is wrong. I imagine God has already brought a certain circumstance or two to your thoughts. Being honest with ourselves is the first step. Be brave and take responsibility for your actions. Then repent and ask God to show you where you can give selfless love. Write down a list if you need to and begin to work on them one by one. ♥ Cherie

Day 7 ~ Love is not Self Seeking

_____

_____

_____

_____

_____

_____

_____

_____

_____

_____

_____

_____

_____

_____

_____

_____

_____

_____

_____

_____

_____

_____

_____

_____

_____

_____

_____

_____

_____

_____

"But for those who are self-seeking and who reject the truth and follow evil, there will be wrath and anger." - Romans 2:8 (NIV)

Chapter 8

Love Is Not Easily Angered

"Let all bitterness and wrath and anger and clamor
and slander be put away from you, along with all
malice. Be kind to one another, tenderhearted,
forgiving one another, as God in Christ forgave you."
-Ephesians 4:31-32 (ESV)

God does not want us to proceed with anger in our hearts and yet we do from time to time. Do you get mad at inanimate objects because they don't work the way you think they should? Are you easily angered by the people around you? Does your first response to them tend to be full of frustration, a lack of patience-maybe even wrath- testing their love for you? We know you don't want to be like this -stuck in a continual rotation of frustration with everyone and everything around you.

Israel really tested God's love for them at Sinai in Exodus 32:1-8. The KJV states in verses 9-11 that God was so angry with them He calls them a "stiff-necked people." They tested His love again in the wilderness in Deuteronomy 9. Pay special attention to vs 22-23 where we see God's anger towards them building. Take a moment to read these passages, then ask yourself this question: can I see myself in the Israelites' responses to God?

God loves Israel. They are His chosen people. Although He met their every need, they continually provoked His wrath by their angry responses. What was missing in their responses to Him? They were lacking the characteristics of love.

Today's Challenge:

Are you angry with God or others over a certain circumstance? Think through the situation and write down what leaps at you. Take a few moments to meditate on this one incident and ask God how you could have responded differently. Then take the steps to repair the relationship. Choosing love over anger is always the best decision. Peter tells us in 1 Peter 4:8 why this characteristic of love is so important. "Above all, love each other deeply, because love covers over a multitude of sins." (NIV) ♥ Cherie

Day 8 ~ Love is not easily Angered

_____
_____
_____
_____
_____
_____
_____
_____
_____
_____
_____
_____
_____
_____
_____
_____
_____
_____
_____
_____
_____
_____
_____
_____
_____
_____
_____
_____
_____
_____
_____
_____

"Above all, love each other deeply, because love covers
over a multitude of sins."

-1 Peter 4:8 (NIV)

Chapter 9

Love Keeps No Record of Wrongs

"He will again have compassion on us; he will tread our iniquities under foot. You will cast all our sins into the depths of the sea." -Micah 7:19 (ESV)

God keeps no record of wrongs!

Are you a list maker? I am. Lists on paper, lists on my computer, lists in my head. Grocery lists, to-do lists, honey-do lists, Christmas lists....you get the idea.

Have you found yourself making lists of the sins that have been committed against you? I did. For years. I rarely committed those lists to paper. Usually I kept those lists tucked safely away in the dark corners of my thoughts, all but forgotten until the next time someone "did me wrong." In an instant, that checklist would come racing to the forefront of my thoughts and I suddenly faced a difficult decision: would I remember all of the blameworthy actions of that person and stack this latest misdeed on the scale of their wrongdoing or would I look at the situation in front of me as a distinct event that needed independent evaluation? (Just a disclaimer to clear up any potential confusion: I'm in no way suggesting that you should overlook anything that threatens your safety or the safety of your children.)

I frequently used this argument with the Lord: "But God, (fill in name here) does this **all the time**. When are you going to speak to them and hold them accountable for their behavior? I'm tired of always being the one to have to make the right choice."

Unfailingly, the Lord would remind me of the parable of the unmerciful servant in Matthew 18:21-35. Would I want to hold another accountable for their small transgression against me and run the risk of having the Lord repay me for all of my sins? My knees go weak at the thought of having to answer for each of my countless sins!

Another verse that the Lord has spoken to my heart repetitively is 1 Peter 4:8, which says, "Above all, love each other deeply, because love covers over a multitude of sin." (NIV)

We are called to let God's perfect love flow through us and cover a multitude of sin. It doesn't seem fair. It *isn't* fair. But it's God's justice; justice that gives us what Jesus paid for rather than what we deserve. Oh, the gratitude and relief I experience when someone lets their love cover my sin!

Over the past twenty years, the Lord has consistently spoken to me in this area. I'm happy to report that I've made great strides in extending grace to others. It has been a hard-fought battle, but I know that it remains an area that requires vigilance so I don't have a relapse!

Some relationships are harder to do this in than others. For many of us, it is more difficult with our spouse or other family members because a stronghold has been built in this area. We have to learn from our experiences with others without holding their mistakes against them. This takes the power of the Holy Spirit being made manifest in our thoughts, words, and actions.

We must remember that His compassion crushes our sins under His feet and puts them at the bottom of the sea. How grateful I am for that! I'm grateful for even more than that: He sent JESUS to pay for our sins. Romans 3:22 says that we have righteousness from God that comes through faith in Jesus Christ. This is not an excuse to sin freely without thought of consequences, but a reminder that God is compassionate and merciful to us and, as His children, we need to display that same compassion and mercy.

Today's Challenge:

Thank God for the grace you have received. He isn't holding your sin against you!

Do you keep a record of wrongs others have committed against you? Do you "rehearse" (in your heart or with your friends) all of the bad/mean/awful things that you see in the lives of others and look at them through the filter of those wrong things or do you see others as God does...with righteousness that comes through faith in Jesus Christ? That list-making can become a habit for us if we do not guard ourselves against that temptation. Assigning blame is so easy, as it can make us feel self-righteous and free of responsibility. If you have given into that temptation, it's time to repent!

Ask the Lord to help you to see others as He sees them. Ask Him to anoint you to cover their sin with His love flowing through you. It might be challenging, but it will be worth it!

Do you feel that someone has such a list against you? Ask the Lord to change their heart about "record keeping" and trust that the Lord will make that change. In the meantime, model the behavior you would like to receive. Because, really, isn't that what God has done for us? ♥ Rebecca

Day 9 ~ Love keeps no records of Wrongs

_____
_____
_____
_____
_____
_____
_____
_____
_____
_____
_____
_____
_____
_____
_____
_____
_____
_____
_____
_____
_____
_____
_____
_____
_____
_____
_____
_____
_____
_____
_____
_____

"He will again have compassion on us; he will tread our iniquities under foot. You will cast all our sins into the depths of the sea." -Micah 7:19 (ESV)

Chapter
10

Love Does Not Delight In Evil

"When wisdom enters your heart, and knowledge is
pleasant to your soul, discretion will preserve you;
understanding will keep you, to deliver you from the
way of evil, from the man who speaks perverse things,
from those who leave the paths of uprightness to walk
in the ways of darkness; who rejoice in doing evil, and
delight in the perversity of the wicked;"
-Proverbs 10-14 (NKJV)

Have you thought or even said the following, "I wish everyone knew who this person truly is," or "If I could, I would shout out all of their wrongs so people will finally know who I know them to be?"

I'm sure many of us would have to raise our hands to answer yes to this question. I have! We all know the drill. Someone does something to wrong us and now they are the enemy. We write their faults on our minds and meditate on every detail. Then satan takes advantage of this by promoting the situation in our minds until each detail gets under our skin. From that point on, we judge everything they do until it drives us so crazy that we are tormented and find joy in waiting for the moment we can blow their cover. Sweet friends, this process is an example of delighting in evil. However, we can find wisdom for this temptation in Isaiah 32:6,

"For the foolish person will speak foolishness, and her heart will work iniquity, to practice hypocrisy, and to utter error against the LORD, to make empty the soul of the hungry, and she will cause the drink of the thirsty to fail." (KJV)

After reading this verse the first time I knew I did not ever want to be her again. This passage scares me. I never again want to utter words against someone because I now understand that by speaking against them I am speaking against my Lord. I don't want to be the reason someone's soul has been emptied and yet, I have been. It breaks my heart to know that I have allowed offense to lead me to lose sight of wisdom and choose to delight in evil instead. I have walked this walk in ignorance and learned some valuable lessons about people, especially women - powerful lessons I don't want to repeat again.

Today's Challenge: STOP!!! It's time to line up our thoughts with God's word. Stop letting satan promote negative thoughts of others in your mind. Doing so promotes sin and brings death into the relationship. But God can break this stronghold.

First: choose to believe what God says is for everyone. God's Word is full of verses that you hold onto as daily reminders of who you are in Christ. Those same verses were written for the people you are struggling with. Receive the same verses for those individuals as you do for yourself.

Second: think about their good qualities and practice the art of praise. Choose to only speak good of them and not evil. Satan is going to tempt you to do otherwise, but stand strong because God wants to use you in this person's life.

Third: pray for them. Something beautiful happens in our hearts when we pray for our enemies. The hardness melts away and we are able to get past the hurts and begin to forgive.

These three steps, though not easy at first, will free you in this area. God once said to me, "Cherie, I didn't just die for your sins, I died for the sins that were committed against you." What better way to break a stronghold than to realign your heart with God's and start doing the complete opposite of what you have done for so long. When God is invited into the circumstances, all things become new. ♥ Cherie

Day 10 ~ Love does not delight in Evil

_____

_____

_____

_____

_____

_____

_____

_____

_____

_____

_____

_____

_____

_____

_____

_____

_____

_____

_____

_____

_____

_____

_____

_____

_____

_____

"Stop letting satan promote negative thoughts of others in your mind. Doing so promotes sin and brings death into the relationship." -Cherie Zack

Chapter
11

Love Rejoices With the Truth

"Jesus answered, 'I am the way and the truth and the life. No one comes to the Father except through me.'"
John 14:6 (NIV)

Have you ever experienced a contrast between the truth of your experience and the truth of the Word of God? I have.

Oxford American Dictionaries states that "true" means "in accordance with fact or reality." When I come up against that conflict between experience and the Word, I find that I have to make a decision concerning which truth to believe. Will I choose the "reality" of my circumstances or the truth of God's Word? Will I choose to believe what God's Word says about me and others, or will I let past and present experiences define what I believe to be true? Often that is a difficult choice to make because I have to deliberately override what my senses and knowledge (my "natural mind") tell me is the logical, and usually negative, anticipated outcome of my situation.

When that decision has to be made, I remember what Jesus said of following his teaching in John 8:32,

"Then you will know the truth, and the truth will set you free." Now that is truth worth rejoicing over!

Jesus is the way and the truth and the life, God's Word made flesh. I have to choose to rejoice in the truth of God's Word *no matter what* because it is the one true thing in life.

This verse is how I reconcile difficult situations that doesn't line up with truth of God's Word:

> *"And we know that in all things God works for the good of those who love him, who have been called according to his purpose." -Romans 8:28 (NIV)*

Trusting the Lord is primary. He knows what we need and He's already provided it: the truth of the One, True and Living God!

Today's Challenge:

Are you struggling to see something worth rejoicing about in your life? The challenge today is to choose to rejoice with the truth...to know the truth about God, about ourselves, about others, and about our circumstances. Rejoice about your spiritual reality...not be discouraged by the negative things you can see.

If you're not certain what the Bible says, research the Word! The Bible overflows with God's promises for you and hope for His provision for you in every circumstance.

The truth is that no matter WHAT you are facing, God works ALL THINGS for the good of those who love him and are called according to His purpose. That's us, dear sisters! Choose to rejoice with that truth today and, like me, you just might find that your emotions begin to line up with that choice to rejoice!

♥ Rebecca

Day 11 ~ Love rejoices in the Truth

"And we know that in all things God works for the good of those who love him, who have been called according to his purpose." -Romans 8:28 (NIV)

Chapter 12

Love Always Protects

"But the Lord is faithful, who will establish you and guard (protect) you from the evil one."
-2 Thessalonians 3:3

Rebecca and I teach a lot on this subject, mostly because it tends to come up often. When someone has hurt us the last thing we want to do is protect them. There are those moments when someone we love says or does the wrong thing. We are stung by the situation and tend to seek an apology or at least try to make them understand what they have done. We judge them for the incident and turn cold towards them. The worst case scenarios cause us to delete this person from our lives. However, God is calling us to a higher level of accountability with Him concerning how we respond to this kind of hurt. Love requires us to protect them because His loves protects us.

Maybe God is stirring your heart toward someone right now and the very thought of turning back to them causes your tummy to turn in knots. I have felt those same knots. It's through this kind of trial I have learned a very important lesson that God continues to teach me in my everyday life. I had to learn to become a "safe place to land" for those I have a relationship with.

Proverbs 17:17 states, *"A friend loves at all times, and a brother is born for adversity."*
Some of my deepest relationships are those that were in danger of being cut off because of the pain I endured at their hands. God taught me that love had to rise above my emotions and my pain. This was hard for me because I could reason that I was better off without them. Why face the pain when we can just cut them out of our lives, right? But, if a friend loves at all times (even the really tough ones) then I had to learn to do the same and so do you.

Today's Challenge:

Instead of turning away from the one who has hurt you, allow yourself to be a safe place for them to land. God said "love always protects." There are no loopholes. Sweet sisters, I know you have been hurt. God sees and understands your affliction. Let's think about this. When you are wrong, God is the first to extend grace to you and He's asking you to do the same for others. By choosing grace over affliction you are now protecting your heart from becoming hard and you are protecting the relationship. You're learning to love at all times. This is a very selfless act and a reflection of our Savior. ♥ Cherie

Day 12 ~ Love always Protects

_____

_____

_____

_____

_____

_____

_____

_____

_____

_____

_____

_____

_____

_____

_____

_____

_____

_____

_____

_____

_____

_____

_____

_____

_____

_____

_____

_____

_____

_____

_____

_____

_____

_____

_____

"But the Lord is faithful, who will establish you and guard (protect) you from the evil one." -2 Thessalonians 3:3

Chapter 13

Love Always Trusts

"Trust in the LORD with all your heart and lean not on your own understanding; in all your ways acknowledge him, and he will make your paths straight."   -Proverbs 3:5-6 (NIV)

What is trust? Trust is the firm belief in the reliability, truth, ability, or strength of someone or something. (Definition from Oxford American Dictionaries)

Do you trust others? Often, we withhold trust from a person because we have been hurt by them or by someone else. When we refuse to trust, we are not fully loving them.

Wow! For me, that's a tough pill to swallow. I don't want it to be that way. Withholding trust appears to be a self-preservation technique that will guard my heart from being hurt. But, the truth of the matter is this: when I don't trust, I don't allow God into the situation. So, even if I don't "feel" like trusting someone I'm in relationship with, I must trust in Jesus and resist the temptation to guard my heart from being hurt.

(On the flip side, I'm not suggesting that we should just simply trust everyone we meet, but we should allow the Holy Spirit to reveal to us who is worthy of our trust and who we need to be cautious with, especially in new relationships.)

While not everyone is trustworthy, God is perfectly trustworthy and He will never let you down!

At the beginning of our marriage, I struggled to trust Robert when it came to making important decisions. One day, as I was pouring out my heart to the Lord concerning my lack of trust (all the while accusing Robert of not being trustworthy), the Holy Spirit made this point to me: I might not be able to trust Robert, but I knew how to trust the Lord. He told me that I needed to trust Him to speak to Robert and trust that Robert would obey. For me, that was a key. Obeying that one direction shifted my attention from Robert and put it back where it belongs: The Lord and His service.

It reminds me of the old hymn: "'Tis so sweet to trust in Jesus. Just to take Him at His Word. Just to rest upon His promise. Just to know, 'Thus saith the Lord.' Jesus, Jesus, how I trust Him. How I've proved Him o'er and o'er...Jesus, Jesus, precious Jesus! O, for grace, to trust Him more." (Lyrics by Louisa M.R. Stead)

Today's challenge:

Repent of your lack of trust in the Lord and ask Him to forgive you. Ask God to anoint you to trust others in your life more deeply than you already do. Then make the decision to deliberately trust Jesus in the circumstances of your life and ask for His grace for you while you grow in your ability to trust!

As you meditate on Jesus' trustworthiness, ask the Lord to make you more trustworthy for others. Use the hurts you've endured as stepping stones instead of material for building a wall. You will begin to trust in God and you will develop, too...because God is faithful! ♥Rebecca

Day 13 ~ Love always Trust

_____
_____
_____
_____
_____
_____
_____
_____
_____
_____
_____
_____
_____
_____
_____
_____
_____
_____
_____
_____
_____
_____
_____
_____
_____
_____
_____
_____
_____

"Trust in the LORD with all your heart and lean not on
your own understanding; in all your ways
acknowledge him, and he will make your paths
straight." -Proverbs 3:5-6 (NIV)

Chapter 14

Love Always Hopes

"Now faith is the substance of things hoped for, the evidence of things not seen." -Hebrews 11:1 (KJV)

I can't help but think about this verse when I hear the word hope!

Faith and hope are intertwined. Hope comes as a result of our faith. Faith always precedes our hope. So the question is, do you have the faith to hope for the things you desire but have yet to see come to fruition in your marriage or life in general? There is evidence it's coming if you have hope.

I have a hope that my daughter's seizure disorder is going to be healed. I have hoped for this for many years now. She started having seizures when she was two years old. She is in her twenties and the seizures are still wreaking havoc on her and our family as a whole. But I have HOPE. I hope in God's word that says, *"Surely he hath borne our griefs, and carried our sorrows: yet we did esteem him stricken, smitten of God, and afflicted. But he was wounded for our transgressions, he was bruised for our iniquities: the chastisement of our peace was upon him; and with his stripes we are healed."* -Isaiah 53:4-5 (KJV)

What are you hoping for? A husband to come to salvation? A job to come through to better your finances? Maybe you are hoping to start college and there doesn't seem to be a way for you to go. You could be like me and praying for a loved one's healing. It's time to take a stand. You would not be reading this if God wasn't wanting to do something in your life and in this area of hope. He is stirring you now. Do you need more convincing? Here are some verses you can stand on.

Hope for your future and the future of the ones you love:

"Know that wisdom is such to your soul; if you find it, there will be a future, and your hope will not be cut off." -Proverbs 24:14 (ESV)

"For I know the plans I have for you, declares the LORD, plans for welfare and not for evil, to give you a future and a hope." -Jeremiah 29:11 (ESV)

Hope for what we are believing for but have yet to see:

"For in this hope we were saved. Now hope that is seen is not hope. For who hopes for what he sees? But if we hope for what we do not see, we wait for it with patience." -Romans 8:24-25 (ESV)

"Rejoice in hope, be patient in tribulation, be constant in prayer." -Romans 12:12 (ESV)

"For whatever was written in former days was written for our instruction, that through endurance and through the encouragement of the Scriptures we might have hope." -Romans 15:4 (ESV)

Reason to stand in your Hope:

"The LORD of hosts has sworn, saying, Surely, as I have thought, so it shall come to pass, And as I have purposed, so it shall stand:" -Isaiah 14:24 (NKJV)

"God is not man, that he should lie, or a son of man, that he should change his mind. Has he said, and will he not do it? Or has he spoken, and will he not fulfill it?" -Numbers 23:19 (ESV)

"The LORD your God is in your midst, a mighty one who will save; he will rejoice over you with gladness; he will quiet you by his love; he will exult over you with loud singing." -Zephaniah 3:17 (ESV)

"Jesus said to her, "Everyone who drinks of this water will be thirsty again, but whoever drinks of the water that I will give him will never be thirsty again. The water that I will give him will become in him a spring of water welling up to eternal life." -John 4:13-14 (ESV)

Today's Challenge:

Have you lost your hope? Write down the areas that you have things you have walked away from and commit them once again to God. Then begin to walk in *faith* that God is resurrecting your hope and bringing life into each area once again. Though your circumstances scream to you otherwise, let hope have its way in your thoughts and trust God to bring to fruition the things He has promised.

Day 14 ~ Love always Hopes

"Now faith is the substance of things hoped for, the evidence of things not seen." -Hebrews 11:1 (KJV)

Love Always Perseveres

"So do not throw away your confidence; it will be richly rewarded. You need to persevere so that when you have done the will of God, you will receive what he has promised." -Hebrews 10:35-36 (NIV)

The dictionary defines "persevere" as "to continue in a course of action even in the face of difficulty or with little or no prospect of success." (Definition from Oxford American Dictionaries)

I don't mind the first part of that definition. However, I'm not too crazy about the part that says "with little or no prospect of success. I like to know that what I'm endeavoring to do has a fairly good chance of a favorable outcome.

I think about how God loves each of us. His love for us persevered even when we didn't give much indication that we were going to give Him our hearts. God continued to pursue us, to pour out His love on us, to woo us until we willingly gave Him our hearts.

Do you do the same for others? Do you persevere in loving them, even when they aren't as loving as you would like or when it seems as if your efforts are futile?

If this is difficult for you, remember what James 1:2-4 says, "Consider it pure joy, my brothers, whenever you face trials of many kinds, because you know that the testing of your faith develops perseverance. Perseverance must finish its work so that you may be mature and complete, not lacking anything." (NIV)

Maybe you struggle to persevere in loving someone who has yet to give their heart to the Lord. Remember His persistence to love and pursue you and commit to do the same. You allow the love of God to be made manifest in your life and the lives of others when you love without giving up!

Today's challenge:

Persevere in your love for others. If you have faltered in your efforts to persevere, repent and ask the Lord to strengthen you as you continue to love those God has given you to love with His unending, never-failing love.

Ask God to show you specifically what you can do to express His love that perseveres to others in your life. He wants to pour out His wisdom to you.

Ask the Lord to reveal to you the stumbling blocks to persevering in love toward others. Take authority over those barriers. Don't let the little things in life steal your drive to persevere! ♥ Rebecca

Day 15 ~ Love always Perseveres

_____
_____
_____
_____
_____
_____
_____
_____
_____
_____
_____
_____
_____
_____
_____
_____
_____
_____
_____
_____
_____
_____
_____
_____
_____

"So do not throw away your confidence; it will be richly rewarded. You need to persevere so that when you have done the will of God, you will receive what he has promised." -Hebrews 10:35-36 (NIV)

Chapter 16

Love Never Fails

*"Lift up your eyes to the heavens, look at the earth
beneath; the heavens will vanish like smoke, the
earth will wear out like a garment and its
inhabitants die like flies. But my salvation will last
forever, my righteousness will never fail."*
-Isaiah 51:6 (NIV)

Failure means to fall short of success or achievement in something expected, attempted, desired, or approved. (Definition from Dictionary.com)

Have you noticed that no matter how many times you fail and turn back to your sin, God is always there? This is because God's love cannot fail. He stays the same through every situation. The Apostle John tells us why:

*"For God did not send His Son into the world to
condemn the world, but that the world through Him
might be saved". -John 3:17*

His ultimate purpose for His love expressed toward us is our salvation. He proved His love for us by laying down His only Son's life for ours. It was His ultimate sacrifice.

The word *requirement* has come up often during this challenge. God required a sacrifice to be given as payment for our sins. His unfailing love is so powerful that it transformed a dying world and raised within it new life.

God modeled sacrifice for us. We must follow His example. He requires a sacrifice on our part: we must sacrifice our own will so that His will can be made manifest in our lives and allow His never-failing, unending love to flow through us to others.

Today's Challenge:

Have you ever failed in your efforts to love others? Today, repent of those times you have fallen short of loving others. Receive the forgiveness that God wants to pour out for you. Now, ask the Holy Spirit to anoint you to love the way God loves: without fail!
♥ Cherie & Rebecca

Day 16 ~ Love Never Fails

"For God did not send His Son into the world to condemn the world, but that the world through Him might be saved". –John 3:17

Congratulations!

You have now completed the 16 Day Love Challenge.

We know this has been tough, but you have persevered. We rejoice with you and celebrate your success in following hard after God's own heart!

Each day's challenge has required something from you. You have been asked to change your thinking, lay down your own desires, love the unlovable, pray for your enemies, become a safe place to land in the face of pain, let go of anger, and let God's love flow through you consistently.

Continue to apply everything you have learned to your love for God and others. Implementing these principles will change you *and* your relationships, enabling you to thrive as the woman God designed you to be.

Cherie & Rebecca

About The Authors

Cherie Zack is the founder of The Imperfect Wives. She has been ministering to women for more than 10 years. She is a certified Biblical counselor in the areas of Marriage and Family and women's ministry. As well as being the founder of The Imperfect Wives, in 2010 Cherie was appointed Director of the South Carolina AG District Council Women's Ministry department where she serves more than 100 pastors and women's ministry groups. She also serves as a board member for The Jubilee Market a ministry that is teaching girls the skills they need to flourish in life after being rescued from human trafficking.

Cherie is seeking a bachelor's degree in psychology with an emphasis in Christian counseling through Liberty University. She is passionate about her marriage, family and women's ministry and loves every minute of each! Cherie and Bill have been married for 19 years and they have 4 children.

Rebecca LeCompte is a self-proclaimed "recovering perfectionist." Throughout her life, she has wrestled with the desire to be perfect in all things while realizing that she is entirely imperfect. After walking with

Jesus for many years, Rebecca is finally at peace (mostly) about being so much less than perfect. Through her weaknesses, Rebecca has seen *God's* perfection, beauty, strength and wisdom made manifest in her life and the lives of her family in countless ways...and she's so grateful!

Rebecca has been married to Robert, the love of her life, for over twenty-three years. They have three children, Nathaniel, a college student, Jesse, who is in high school, and Sophia, an elementary student. The LeComptes have been a homeschool family for over fourteen years. This flexible lifestyle has meshed beautifully with the military lifestyle they enjoy as Robert serves as a chaplain in the United States Navy.

Rebecca first expressed her desire to teach at the tender age of four, when she would come home from kindergarten and teach her dolls everything she learned at school. Teaching has remained a strong desire in her heart throughout her life, as she has taught toddlers to adults in a variety of settings. Although she enjoys teaching a range of subjects, Rebecca is most passionate about teaching others about the goodness and grace of God and how to develop a deeper, more intimate relationship with Jesus that results in victorious living. As a partner with *The Imperfect Wives,* Rebecca has delighted in seeing God move in the hearts and lives of women as they seek His wisdom for their personal journeys and for their marriages. Rebecca serves with Rob, full time, in their ministry *Internal Instruments*.

Connect with us here:

Cherie

The Imperfect Wives website

Facebook

The Imperfect Wives Club

Imperfect Wives Radio

Email

Rebecca

Internal Instruments

Facebook

Website

Email

Made in the USA
Monee, IL
16 October 2021

80114862R10069